UNSTOPPABLE

An electrifying collection of short stories

that will change your life!

Presented by Rachel E. Bills

Published by Women of Virtue Publishing Co.

ISBN-13:978-1-7349360-1-8

Dedication From The Authors...

La Wanda Marrero

I dedicated this chapter of past hurts and healing to my family, friends, and community. I am proud to say on my journey I have been met with hardships and triumph yet, here I stand a sinner in servitude not on my accord but, by The Lord's grace. After publishing, Alice N Crackland I realized writing was an essential tool in acknowledging, accepting overcoming the challenges I as a child and in my adult life. It is my belief others can also benefit from learning to express themselves through the art of writing and pretense. As I continue to march toward victory, I know that I am not alone and neither are you, the reader. I am amazed at the love and responses I have seen as I have traveled through spiritual experiences and the peeling of yesterday's emotional turmoil of hurt and rejection. In search of my true self I have impacted many lives both positive and negative. Having firsthand, knowledge of family dynamic and dysfunction, I embrace and value my experiences. The road to redemption is a bridge to healing and I am on it.

Rachel E. Bills

I dedicate this chapter first and foremost to my Father in Heaven who turned my test into a testimony and my trial into triumph. The one whom I owe my life to and who gave me Jesus; the one whom I serve with my life. Thank you for my purpose!

I dedicate this chapter to each of my children; Ragene (my oldest), Dajanae (my second), Dandre(my son) and Mikaylah (my youngest). I can only hope I can live up to be the mother they can be proud of. I love you all to the moon and back!

I dedicate this chapter to my father and mother for giving me life. To my siblings and the boat load of nieces and nephews I've been blessed to have. I love each of you I pray you live your life to the fullest!

Lastly, I dedicate this chapter to all the individuals who have struggled to accept their mistakes and move on. Those who have been bitter, angry and broken from past trauma. You are not alone. If God saw me through it, He will see you through it too! You are UNSTOPPABLE!!

Sharnice Perryman

I'm dedicating my chapter to all my ex-husbands. They taught me to become better and never bitter. They taught me that with every break up comes a breakthrough. I learned that through loss and abandonment comes inevitable growth and gain. I have become determined to never be found where I was left.

Tene Kyles

I am dedicating my chapter to the little girl in me and every little girl who feels like they don't have a voice. My chapter will speak on behalf of those who cannot be heard. Proverbs 31:8.9 says that I am to "Speak up for those who cannot speak for themselves; for the rights of all who are destitute."

Shantel Greer

I am dedicating this chapter first to God. Whom helped me see the light and kept me strong through this journey. Second, I would like to dedicate this chapter to Mari K for helping me uncover true facts. To My two daughters whom supported me, with their heads up high. When mines was hung down low.

TABLE OF CONTENTS

Dedications from the Authors

Introduction

We would like to say thank you for making "Unstoppable" your book choice. Readers from all walks of life and personal persuasions will be inspired by the resiliency of the human spirit and filled with compassion for these authors. As I reflect on my early writing challenges which were mostly journals, I never imagined I would become a published author and per my discussion with my fella authors in this book compilation neither did they. I find it amazing how life can take a completely different direction than expected. I believe destiny will always supersede our personal desires as the end draws neigh. (meaning as we mature and age).

The purpose of "Unstoppable" is to encourage those who have struggled with living their destiny and relentless search for the truth of their best selves. Our mission is to bring hope to the lives of those who have been through provocative dark journeys and trials, often stagnating or delaying the fulfillment of their purpose.

Each of the women who shared their captivating stories are strong, mighty women who never gave up regardless of what they were faced with; abuse, abandonment, rejection and demonstrated the amazing ability to rise above the devastating confusion of being abused by those who were supposed to love and protect them.

We are all overcomers, facing life on life's terms and this also means you (the reader) too. Life is not about the start nor how your story begins. It's the miraculous effect of how you lived, impacted, and how your story ends.

I don't believe you blindly stumbled onto this book by happenstance. But it was a divine appointment "just for you" to read, explore, and find your (internal) light. To gain a renewed understanding of compassion, and respect for yourself and others.

I pray as you journey into all the victorious stories you allow them to saturate your mind, body, and spirit so you will realize how "Unstoppable" you are.

Blessings!

La Wanda Marrero
Author, Mother

"Past Hurts"

Inspired by Auntie Caroline.

Recreation or re -creation: choose….

That was then, this is now. That was there, this is here. The appetite wants delights, but the soul needs purpose. We search for gratification and fulfillment and find ourselves in the most compromised and self-destructive positions and act as if we are shocked at the outcome. I was sharing this aspect of thought with a male friend named Rasta. He responded by stating, "You lay down in the mud you get muddy." My response was, "No, you bring the mud with you."

My identified crisis? Thinking I'm something, learned I'm nothing…. Especially without Christ.

All my selves: Jerus, Wanda, Jarasta, Chickee, and…. Whosoever shall believe can become transformed, be the change from the past and reflect the newness of life.

There is a void that lives on the inside of me where past hurts used to house. I'm diligently trying to feel and fill that void ("You have to feel it to heal it.") with the love of the Lord because He has shown me Himself through His love yet again. Because of my accomplishments, people say You deserve it. I tell myself No I don't, but He did it for me anyway. This is the rawness of my life and my walk with God. I'm sharing it as I live it in hopes that someone else will also find themselves in the trueness of their real selves and the richness of the Lord.

Because you the reader are traveling on this journey with me in my rawness, prayerfully you may gain perspective on your past hurts. When you read this slogan, *Pen & Pad Moment!* remember to take serious note of it because it will assist in identifying who you are and how you continue to contribute to the hurt that returns to you repeatedly, sometimes disguised. The energy you provide becomes the core source to fuel past hurts.

I'm transitioning into a new life. There is no space for past hurts to dwell in comfort. I don't have to rely on those past hurts to sustain, justify, or motivate me to move forward. I cannot stagnate with emotional attacks and move forward simultaneously.

Although I want to just sit back and bask in God's love, I am called to do something more. So, I'm restless and often have many sleepless nights. Familiar spirits, once they leave me, search for another place to dwell. If they cannot find a resting place, they come back to me. If you are blinded by your emotions, you are vulnerable. Past hurts come in different seductive forms. However, if you are spiritually in tune with the word of God and can recognize the word of God you will know when they have arrived. "I see you Devil, and I'm not falling for that again." This can be a learning experience, an opportunity to use the glory of God's love to fill and feel and heal the void of past hurts.

Another side of familiar Spirits known to me, the believer, is that I am so used to God taking such good care of me, I have found myself taking his goodness for granted. I was blinded and unaware of my role in situations and I pointed fingers and blame. For example, I have been in several failed relationships. I realize and now accept I initiated those relationships and those men were who they were long before I inserted myself into their lives. I couldn't see them for who they were because I had no idea of who I was. I did not understand my value not only as a woman but God's daughter. I was living in and out of my imagination.

I had unrealistic expectations in these men and my ability to change them with my wonderful artificial loving self. I put my desire for them to change who they were to fit my idea of who I wanted them to be. This played out in various forms of drugs, sex, violence, scars, and babies with different last names. Finding what I thought to be love in all the wrong places, I went through years of torment feeling rejected over and over. It had become a part of who I was, and it is was not so easy to shake.

I now know it was connected to being molested by my uncle at an early age. To learn more about that story read my book, Alice N Crackland. Since childhood into adulthood different personalities with alternate names evolved just to keep myself safe. Where I felt I was weak in one area I had to bring another part of myself into being strong, and when I was too strong and overbearing, I needed to be more sensitive. Then I had to hustle and form an I-don't-care attitude. I had to develop yet another personality. Now I'm just trying to incorporate all of who I am into one being, God's child living in the abundance of life.

I'm pretty sure people who read my story or know me wonder, what is she talking about? She's accomplished quite a few things: she is a survivor, published author, has a master's degree, raised a family, purchased a home, steady employment, and has a nonprofit. She's been productive! I say Yes, that's right, I agree, but those are works (outside projects) that kept me busy. But I'm talking about a real relationship with The Lord and seeing myself in my raw form, the areas of my life that don't please me or God.

those spaces I often try not to think about because of fear and shame of what I will learn and see about me. This is a Pen & Pad Moment!

When I allow The Lord to lead, I can live a spiritually fed life with abundant promise. This has nothing to do with earthly things. It's important to me to obtain *God's wisdom*. I seek it from God because my version and yours are tainted. Past hurt rejections show up often in my life to re-traumatize me. So, I hold on tight to the word of God like Jacob/Israel wrestled and held on to the Angel until the Lord blessed him. It changed not only his name but his life. Jesus was rejected and if I am created in His likeness it only makes sense that I am rejected too. Now I'm spilling this out like it was simple for me to grasp, but it was not! I'm getting delivered right now as I share it. Why now? Because I'm giving myself permission to release it to God and accept my healing. Thank you, Lord. Rejection took life in me at an early age. I have grown up with it. Yes, I was robbed of my innocence which affected my ability to choose and make appropriate decisions. I even came to realize I rejected myself, not understanding, not being protected, and not talking about what happened until I was in my late 30's. Now I am 60 and finally I have allowed God, Yes, I said allowed God, because you must ask God to come into your heart and willingly allow Him to open your eyes, ears, and, heart which are the gates to our souls. God will connect, soothe, and deliver you from those ongoing thoughts and feelings of past hurts in all forms like employment, partnerships, relationships, parenthood, friendships, and yes rejections. We are still in a Pen & Pad Moment!

Place your past hurts here for healing. I saw myself step into the deliverance realm where I had been rejected but was now healed and it no longer was important how or what happened, only that it is used for God's Glory. Yes, to God be the Glory because of me sharing my rejection others can take courage. Now surely, I have repented and given my heart to the Lord on numerous occasions. I accept God, or I give God my burdens, my aches and pains of life, I accept his forgiveness and deliverance but then when that core of rejection returns, looking like the finest thing that ever walked the earth, in all of its attractiveness and splendor directed toward my fleshly desires, I must be honest here. I convinced myself that I needed that core of rejection to survive because I was lonely, and no one was looking my way. I'm shedding tears right now because I realize how could I ever think that I was alone when I have God and his power.

I gain my strength in the Lord and the people he places and circumstances that he provides for me in whatever journey I'm on. My sister/cousin Yolo has a spot called the Healing Center. We have grown up together, had some differences in and on our journeys, but she has coined a wonderful phrase: The babies are leaping. This term refers to Jesus and John the Baptist being in the wombs of their mothers and bearing witness to the truth to one another and their purpose to come. So, I dedicate this part of the chapter to her and the wisdom of God that resides in her. Iron sharpens iron.

Yolo shared with me that we must be willing to heal especially in the areas of relationships. It was difficult to hear and digest because sometimes my thoughts and ideas of how I think and feel about past relationships have been with me so long. It is a miserable comfort because it is so familiar. It's been my perspective, my experience, my safety even if it's distorted.

So, I let my guard down as she ministered to me. Yolo said, "Wanda, I am a woman, and when I searched for healing, I listened to a man's perspective. Yes, it's about women's healing but what about the off-spring, the children? In order to understand separateness, we also must understand the things that we have in common as humans such as the truth-- the truth is the truth and has no gender. If we start at the truth, it's the same foundation for everybody. We can choose to move forward and work together even though we are different. It's about understanding how you and the way you live life impacts others and how others life impact yours even though we work very hard to deny it. Families need healing but all members must be willing. Sometimes one unit of the family, woman, man, or child works on healing but if they don't all work together it is a lost game. Pen & Pad Moment!

People make statements like, I am grown, I do what I want to do, nobody can tell me what to do, you are trying to control me, when the truth is pointed out to them. There is a lack of realistic understanding that we are connected. You don't get here by yourself and even when you're disconnected you look for ways to be connected to something. The babies were leaping as I reflected on my life and my children and the past hurts. I felt as if I unwarily passed it on like a generational curse. I pictured a flash of me giving myself to the Lord. The children and I went to church as a family and they had the opportunity to witness and partake of the transformation. It was a healing.

Yolo went on to say, "Don't un-employ faith, faith has a job to do, Wanda." God's wisdom will talk to you when you need it through the people of God. As she continued to minster on, I felt the cutting away and shedding of past hurts of family transparency, secrets, and truth avoidance. I asked myself what satanic forces inside of me are blocking me? Do I want to be completely healed? She said, "Oh taste and see that He is good!" I nearly jumped out of my seat as the babies were leaping. The veil had been torn there

14

was no need for a priest. Come to God, the Lamb for yourself and receive by faith, no handicap salvation.

Most important part of this Pen & Pad Moment! about past hurts is God will use nouns and pronouns, people, places, and things, he's, she's, they's and them's to reach and teach.

By La Wanda Marrero

La Wanda Marrero

Rachel E. Bills
Author, Personal Development &
Writing Coach

"Letting Go of Me"

You might be asking, what type of title is this? How can I let "me" go? Aren't we taught never to let go of ourselves? Yes, we are. We are taught it and we should never let go of who we are. But this title is saying something different. It's saying to let go of that part of you that is hindering you. That part that is keeping you from moving forward in your life. I know it's hard to believe, but sometimes we can be as much harm (or more) to ourselves than the next person. For years I have struggled with bitterness, rage and depression. Even when I thought I was rid of these things; they would sneak back up into my life and cause me to stagger. Even when I prayed and asked God to release and heal me, it would pop up. It caused me to have problems making and keeping people in my life, creating business relationships, being able to communicate with my family, children and co-workers. It was really bad. I could feel myself gasping as if I was being smothered. But thank God for revelation.

Soon I realized that those issues were internal and that they kept coming back because even though I had moved on from the experience and the things (and people) who contributed to my suffering, I had not forgiven the one person who I felt was still responsible...me. I was still angry at myself for allowing things to happen in my life. See it's different when things happen that is beyond your control. People can say, "Baby, it wasn't your fault. It wasn't you; it was so and so's fault." But what about when you have contributed to your repeated downfall? Well, that was my situation. Time and time again I made the wrong decisions that lead to suffering for me and my children. It took me getting tired of the lack in my life and fearing that my children would go down the same path. I had to make up to stop hindering my own future.

18

Today, I am in a greater place than I have been in a very long time. I am excelling and doing things now that helps me live the best version of myself.

So, how did do it? By letting go of me. That part of me that caused me to relive past trauma in my life. That part that caused me to hold unforgiveness over my own head. That part of me that attracted and toxified relationships that were unhealthy. Once I let go of that part of Rachel, I was able to begin living a life of peace and prosperity.

I don't know you or your situation but if you've read up to this part of my chapter then that means you have experienced and can relate to my story in some way. If that's true, you too are on your way to healing. I just want to encourage you not to give up on you or the process that God maybe taking you through. Believe me, I know it's hard but the victory after the healing is far greater than any suffering we encounter.

Dangers of not letting go

As I said previously, I allowed depression, anger and

19

bitterness to overtake me. Yes, I was hurt but it's one thing to be hurt and another to keep making bad discussions. They say insanity is to keep doing the thing and expecting a different result. If that's true then I confess. Even when God lead me into one direction, somehow, I would detour and go back. I would resist the very unction in my spirit until I find myself in deep trouble. I know you may not have expected to read this chapter. Call it my confession, but if you do have or had some issues with disobedience then keep reading. This is your chance to hear from someone who has lived a life of the "prodigal son (well daughter in my case)". See the dangers of not putting yourself in check is missed opportunities and blessings. I can't tell you how many missed and delayed blessings I've let go and I couldn't let go. One in particular is when I didn't show up to get an apartment and the result was my children and I not having a place to live for a year. The strain that I put on my family was horrific.

Not letting go will cause generational curse for your children, who imitate what they see. This is a known fact and taught in Child Development courses. The bible says, "Train up a child in the way they should go: and when he is old, he will not depart from it." (Proverbs 22:6)(KJV) The thing is, we are training our kids not only with our words, but more so with our actions. What we do in front of our kids gets rooted in them. My kids witnessed violence and tantrums and so they mimicked it when things went wrong. It took a lot to get them through it. But even to this day, when my ex and I have a disagreement my kids become tense. As parents, we are to make sure our children developmental stages are healthy. But the hard truth is sometimes we sacrifice our kids' life for our own happiness. When I first heard those words, a lump formed in my throat because it wasn't just the sad truth for me, it was my realty. Because there were times when I could have ended their suffering, I didn't. It just it took me so long to see the truth because I would be too busy putting the blame on other people instead of looking at my own contribution.

Another danger of not letting go, is illness. Illness could be mental, physical or emotional. From simple symptoms like headache and body aches to full blown depression. I've experiences all, both and everything in between.

Hitting Rock Bottom

According to addiction specialists, there is a point in which the addict has nowhere to turn. They have lost any and everything that had value in their life. This is known as hitting "rock bottom" and it is at this point, they (the addict) is forced to admit they have a problem and begin seeking help to change. These specialists also say, everyone has their own rock bottom. This is significant because everyone has their own set of values and beliefs. What may devastate me to lose me be a breeze for you.

The rock bottom concept doesn't just apply to addiction. I continued to rebel against warnings to make some changes in my life. Then, I hit my rock bottom. I was celebrating my birthday and decided to take the kids to Tahoe. This would be my second time in the snow and my kids' first. We were all excited about going to Tahoe, not only for snow fighting, but just to get away from our normal life. We bought weather appropriate clothes, all the personal care items, snacks for the road-trip and even snow chains. Our family was under so much stress without realizing it and I just wanted to take my kids and run. So, I did. Even if it was just for a weekend, I was planning to leave everything behind at least for that moment and enjoy myself with my kids. Yeah, the weekend trip would make my life's problems go away.

The trip was nice. There, we saw lots of beautiful scenery of mountains covered in snow. It was epic. We took pictures that looked like those on postcards. We listened to music and played our favorite road trip games.

After checking into the hotel, we went for a drive around the town. Streets, lawns and rooftops were filled with snow. It was beautiful, but I still couldn't help feeling pressure in my chest. I had been under a lot of stress; my personal life was a hot mess and I started seeing it take effect on my kids. I worried that my son (15 at the time) would get into trouble, because he started leaving with friends, I've prevented him from hanging out with. My daughters were constantly bickering until I yelled for them to quit. But every

23

day it was the same scenario. I won't get into my marital issues. Let's just say divorce was inevitable. So, all this was happening in my life, but I had to keep going. I refused to look like a failure. I wouldn't give my haters and naysayers the advantage of watching me meltdown. No, I did what I always do, run! Run from my problems and ignore that I was being affected. Even though the pain in my chest was a constant reminder of my harboring bitterness, unforgiveness, anger (now rage). I know I should've heeded to the warning that my body was telling me, but I chose to swallow the lump in my throat (as I held back the tears of my sorrow) and ignored the pain in my chest (from all the built-up stress).

I continued to drive and look at my kids. As long as they were happy, I no longer mattered. I felt I deserved whatever pain I was feeling. My feelings were beyond hurt, they were ruined. I was ruined. So, I kept driving until we came across mountains of snow. We had snow fights (just as we planned). My kids looked like kids with no problems, no issues. I wanted to capture the moment, so I took pictures. I also forgot about my problems until the heaviness in my chest came back, this time a little harder.

After the snow fight, we went to get ice cream and the kids went snow boarding. More pictures. This time I stayed in the car. I didn't want my inner issues to ruin a good time. The heaviness was breath-taking, but my kept going. I fought through it like I've always done. After getting ice cream, my son looked at me as we headed toward the car. I remember walking up and it seem like it was taking forever to get to the car. My son didn't say anything, he just walked by my side as if he could feel my pain. I didn't want to have to share that burden so I told him everything was alright. Back at the hotel, the lobby had a huge wood burning fireplace that was perfect during the current snow weather. And the room was beautiful; a cabin theme with double queen beds. We could see snow everywhere through sliding glance doors that lead from the room to the back of the hotel. So, the girls decided to go out and enjoy it. My son went with them asking if I needed anything. "Rest" was my response. I told them to go and I would take a nap while they were out. Yes, rest is what I needed. I figured I would feel better after a good nap.

After they left, I laid back on the bed and rested my head on the (what felt like goose-down) comfortable pillows. It didn't take long to feel myself fading out.

About two hours later I woke up. The kids were sitting on the second bed watching TV.

I had been in oblivion, but woke up just to feel the pain again. This time it was severe. I sat up on the side of the bed and placed my hand on my chest. I could feel my heart racing. But that was normal because lately I was having anxiety attacks. But this was a little different. I tried to take deep breaths to relax, but it felt like something was closing my windpipe every time I tried. What was happening? I finally told my kids that I needed to go to the hospital.

Acknowledging Your Part

Here is where I could write in my story all the things that people have done to me. The abuse, the betrayals, the false accusations, hurt, pain and so on and so on. But I'm not. This is where I make a confession instead. Where I share how I stopped

26

blaming others for my continued suffering. See, even though my pain started with someone hurting my feelings, it was me who continued to relive it. I kept myself as the victim of my past and brought it into my present. I carried it with me to every home I lived, every job I worked at, every city I moved in to, and every relationship I established. It was me. I don't know when it happened, but I had given up the fight. I fight to defeat anything that tried to change me as the true person I am. And instead of fighting, I just ran. Everything I had buried, had taken it's toll on me mentally and physically because I chose to ignore the signs. But that two-day hospital stay, monitors and tests changed my mind. Doctors telling me I had a heart attack. All I could think about were my kids and not wanting to leave them.

I was watching one of TD Jakes's sermons on YouTube and he said "Don't give up the fight". He referred to the story about David and how Goliath underestimated David because he didn't look like a warrior. I remember him saying so adamantly, "Fight anyway! No matter what just fight!" So, at that point I made a

27

decision to face my fears and my pain head on. I had decided not to allow people in my life to treat me less than how I treat myself. Let me tell you, it was not easy. I had to do some soul-searching and admit that I allowed myself to be taken advantage of even when I knew it was not right and I didn't say or do anything. I was attracted to reckless relationships. Reckless because it's a one-way trip to nowhere. Being in the company of those who can't help themselves, let alone, be able (or even willing) to help you.

For many years I couldn't understand why my life was never quite in order. I say quite because I would work so hard for something and lose it so quickly. For example, every time I tried get things in order at home with my kids it would end in chaos. I would take two steps forward just to take three steps back. Never really content, happy or fulfilled. But yet, I would continue on with the same pattern; choosing things (and people) who put me down instead of build me up. And at the end of it all there really wasn't anyone to blame but myself.

Forgiveness

"Forgiveness is never about the other person." You can say that again. Forgiveness is an internal factor that contributes to how you see the world and yourself. What I mean by that is, you will never be able to see that aspect of the world (the good part) while harboring unforgiveness. There will always be an invisible shield that nothing or nobody can get through and while it may get the negative things from entering, it will also keep out the good things. I lived with unforgiveness for years and during that time I couldn't really give my kids that part of a loving mother that they needed. I tried, but it was really hard. Whenever I got mad at something, it would escalate to another level.

I kept re-living past traumas in my mind over and over. Even when I knew God was telling me to let it go, I wouldn't. I didn't want to. I felt I had the right to hold it against them who hurt me. More so, I was angry at God for allowing it to happen. And even though I was keeping up a good image before others; I call it my "Facebook image", I wasn't happy. Yes, I went to church. Yes, I confess the name of Jesus. But I was still angry. It wasn't until I ended up in that hospital bed that I realize I gave the devil what he wanted…I was killing myself.

I looked back on the years and realized I had isolated myself from family and friends. I turned down so many business opportunities because it required me to really put myself out there and be social. I remember getting so many compliments when I was one of the speakers at a women's conference. After the coordinator of the conference called me and told me how excellent I did, she didn't hear from me for two years. Abandoned those who tried to help me because of those who had torn me down and burned many bridges.

I realized that not only did I have to forgive those who hurt me, but also forgive myself. I had to accept the things I did that contributed to years of stagnation and I had to let that side of me that wouldn't let me forget it, go. This took some time. But I started by talking to God and asking him to forgive me. I asked God to help me to see myself the way He sees me. To help me love myself the way He loves me. And as I began to put my trust more in God and "His" process whether than what I was feeling, the burden got lighter. What keeps me now is that I stay focused on God's purpose in my life. I remember that it's not about me or what I feel, but it's about doing what God has called me to do and connecting with those individuals who were sent to get me there.

The Aftermath

My only son started hanging out with gang bangers, both my daughters wanted nothing to do with marriage. My oldest daughter also struggling with anger issues and her inability to manage it. My second oldest admitted having problems with anger, although she can control it better than her sister. Just hearing her confess how she wants to hit people when they make her angry, was unimaginable for me. Was it that I didn't realize the impact my actions were having on my kids or maybe I didn't just care for a long time? My inability and refusal to stop running back to toxic relationships and behaviors not only hindered me completing goals I had for myself, but nearly destroyed the lives of my kids. But I am

31

grateful we have a God of second chances.

The recovery process has been ongoing. They say trouble is easy, it's getting ourselves out of it, that's hard. But with God and setting boundaries, my kids and I have come a long way. My son stopped hanging out with negative crowds, but I still have to stay on him regarding homework. But I'll take that any day. My second daughter is now working, bought a new car and working on her stock portfolio. My oldest daughter still struggles to get back on track, however she is managing her anger incredibly. Even my youngest is doing well. At 13 she now has her own clothing and cosmetic business (which she created all on her own).

As for me, I am walking in my purpose which is to share with others where I came from so that hopefully it will encourage others that they have the power to change their situation. That, even if we may have made some bad decisions and mistakes contributing to our struggles, our story doesn't have to end there. All we have to do is trust God, forgive ourselves and move on. We are truly unstoppable.

Sharnice Perryman
Author, Pastor

"Victory in the Valley"

If someone would have told me that being homeless for a year was gonna be good for me, I would have thought they were crazy. But sure enough, it was for my good. I had been married for almost a year and God spoke these three words to me; desecrate, eradicate and vindicate. Not knowing that this was God's way of preparing me for what was to come. Although, I don't believe anything could have prepared me for the worst storm of my life. My very own valley experience.

My husband and I married after knowing each other for 3 months. We met online. He was gainfully employed at the time and driving a BMW. Of course, he was a church going God fearing man

33

who said to have had the calling of a Pastor on his life. When he proposed to me, he said that I wouldn't have to want for anything and I believed him. I thought to myself, "He must know exactly what to say to win me over or he must be pretty well off because my wants and needs are endless and costly."

So here I was newly married, living in my dream home, furnished the way I had always wanted my dream home to be furnished. At this time, he is no longer gainfully employed, no longer driving a BMW, but we were walking and living by faith. Our finances were shaky due to his inability to secure another job no matter how hard he tried. However, we were still operating in ministry at what we thought was a good level and capacity. I had such mixed emotions at this time. My emotions ranged from; God I know you are with me to how could my husband allow this to happen to us. Although, God gave me those three words desecrate, eradicate and vindicate, at the time, I did not fathom the gravity of the warning. Nor did I know that I would literally have to walk out those three words in order to get to my purposed place. As a woman of God, I felt that my faith was being tested. However, at the same time, as a wife I felt myself becoming very disappointed and frustrated within my marriage. I was so torn and conflicted in my heart. As women we are taught that our husband is to protect and provide for us as their wife. I did not feel protected or provided for. We are led to believe that we are to place our trust in our husbands and their abilities to make or disallow things to happen. So, with all of these expectations came a huge let down. We weren't even in that house for a full year.

At the time my husband proposed to me, I was not looking to be married. I was happy and content in being single. When we went to church during our short courtship, it was prophesied that he was to be my husband, so I felt that I couldn't argue with God and I happily decided to marry him. Like I said, he had promised that I wouldn't want for anything, so just imagine my devastation when we were facing an eviction. Although I know he had good intentions that did not soften the blow of the devastation. Basically, good intentions don't amount to anything when you are facing a great loss that not only was going to affect me but also my two youngest sons.

By this time, we had had several prophecies that spoke about our purpose, ministry and the calling on both of our lives. People of God were always speaking prosperity over our lives and prophesying about the great ministry that my husband and I would have and that we were going to touch many lives. So, it was hard for me to understand how being homeless was going to fit into the plan of God for our lives. Initially I just could not see that it was all apart of the process. Since then, I have come to learn that Greatness can only come through being processed and our willingness to submit and go through the process. That valley experience was a part of the process. A process is a series of actions, changes or functions that brings about results. It also means to prepare by subjecting to a special process. God was allowing these things to take place to result in what was to be our future ministry. I had heard someone say that, "God works thru events to bring you to your purpose. He will take you from pain to power."

No matter how hard he tried, my husband was not able to secure a job that would enable us to stay in our home. I was working but one income just wasn't enough. The wife in me was getting frustrated while the woman of God in me was determined to keep the faith and I was frantically looking for answers that would help it all make some sense. My thoughts were that he wasn't looking hard and long enough. I didn't believe he was showing enough concern and his attitude appeared to be too casual for what we were facing.. Surely God would not have me and my family out on the streets and surely, He would give us a miracle. He gave me nothing but those three words; desecrate, eradicate and vindicate

Right before the eviction, I went to church and got a confirmation about what was about to take place. The prophet took my hands and said these earth-shaking words to me. He said, "That was of God and this will be of God". Those words shook me to my core. I knew it meant that my marriage and everything that came with it was of God and what I am about to face, meaning the eviction was of God too. Yes, God gave me my husband and my house and now God is allowing me to lose the house. My head was spinning and at the time I just couldn't make any since of me and my family becoming evicted. It was such a harsh reality. I was trying to figure out what that was going to look like? Two ministers of the Gospel homeless. People of faith and power homeless. I had never, up until that time, heard of such a thing ever happening. Later I found out that many of the giants of the gospel had spent some time homeless.

Eradicate means to remove, to get rid of and to uproot. So what God was letting me know is that He was going to remove, get rid of and uproot some things. My first though was this is speaking spiritually. But little did I know he was going to start the process in the natural realm first. As a family, we were removed from our home by the eviction. We were uprooted from the lifestyle we had become accustomed to and all the comforts that came with it. God literally had gotten rid of all of our earthly possessions. We eventually lost everything but the shirts on our backs.

We were in denial and kept the faith all the way till the day the sheriffs came knocking. We had not packed a single box. We made no preparations thinking that God was going to change His mind. I had never allowed my emotions to overtake me. Although I wanted to lash out at my husband and ask him the obvious questions like, how could you let this happen to us? I held my peace. I was torn between trusting in God and still wanting to see my husband pull us out of this situation.

So here we were homeless and this is how we stayed for a whole year. It was 365 days, 12 months and 4 seasons of being displaced. It was this time that I spent in the valley that God was able to strip me from everything I thought I knew about Him. This was the part where we suffered the desecration. Desecrate means to insult the character of someone who considers themselves in a sacred position of purpose; to violate the sanctity of; to profane. Can you imagine the talk of the people who knew that we as ministers were homeless and destitute? They just knew that God was not with us. There is something about being put to an open shame that will bring you into a closer relationship with God. When God becomes the only person that you can rely on, it causes you to turn your face away from stuff and turn your face to Him. It's at that moment you can truly say you know Him intimately.

It was in that valley experience that I came to realize that God is always at work. When I found myself at that crossroad and was faced with one of the biggest trials of my life, and I was at the point of not knowing what to do or where to turn. I developed such a faith and trust in God like never before. It was that valley experience that led me to my own personal promise-land; there was no alternate route. I had to go through it to be right where I am now. A person of empathy and compassion. Two of the most important characteristics that are needed for effective ministry. When we journey through the valley, we must always keep in mind that God will always make a way. He will always give us the victory. You will have many trials and you will cry many tears, there will be friends and family members who will misunderstand you; they will criticize you, talk about you, and judge you unfairly in the valley. We must always keep in mind that God's grace, God's leading, and God's mercy will never fail us. His way may not always be the same as the one we would have chosen. But the valley is necessary to get us to where God wants us to be. Unlike the mountain top, the valley is where we do our struggling. The valley isn't our final destination but God will meet us in the valley.

It was in the valley where God used the tools of desecration and eradication to lead me to my victory of vindication. The lessons that God taught me in the valley has ultimately led me to my divine purpose and has taught me that the valley was my gift. It wasn't easy but I became willing to allow God to work out some things in me and make the necessary changes to be able to go from adversity to victory.

Tene Kyles
Author / Advocate

"It Was Not Your Fault!"

I know from experience that when I was molested growing up I would blame myself. Did I dress too provocative? Did I provoke the abuse? Did I ask for it unknowingly? All these thoughts and ideas ran ramped in my head. I would cry and ask myself, why me? Each time I would have an encounter with the molester, I grew angrier and angrier. After years of molestation, I was beyond angry, confused, scared and broken. I didn't understand how an individual that was supposed to love and protect me from the world could be the one that I needed protecting from. Confused because I didn't really understand what was happening to me. Angry because no one was able to protect me. I had this deep dark secret that I had to keep buried, that I wanted to confess. Can you imagine being a

43

child carrying such a secret around for years? Causing me to be scared because I didn't know what would happen if I did confess this deep secret. Would I be looked at differently? Would people believe me? Would people blame me for what happened? So many questions but no answers. Then the audacity of me not wanting to ruffle any feathers and keep the molester safe and in good standing with the rest of the family.

What was wrong with me? I hated the molestation and wanted it to stop however, I was not brave enough to tell anybody. Why, because I loved this person. He took care of me and my siblings the best he could, put a roof over our heads, put food in our stomach, and clothes on our back. How could I want to get him in trouble, he said he loved us. Who was I to not believe him? I was a young girl, what daddy says is law. What young girl do you know that doesn't want the love of her father? Still, something inside of me was growing. Was it hate?

With each encounter over the years, I realized that the molestation became more perverted. It started off small in a sense.

44

You know just touching my private areas, and fondling my breast. Then it changed where I had to stroke his penis until he got an erection and he ejaculated in my hand. Then the breast sucking began while rubbing on my private part. I didn't know what was happening or how to react to this. I just laid there in fear, stiff as a board, hoping someone walked in and caught him so I didn't have to tell. Encounter after encounter the sexual activities increased, he then began kissing and licking my private part, telling me to open my legs and relax. How in the world was I supposed to relax, I was a young and innocent girl who knew nothing about sexuality. I was a child! However, I was being treated as an adult.

Then, one day, the game changed, and he wanted me to put his penis in my mouth. I kept saying no but eventually he made me do it. I didn't know what I was doing. I just closed my eyes and all I could feel was his penis going back and forth in my mouth. I felt so dirty and remember telling myself: I dare not tell a soul, what an embarrassment this would be if I told this! At a certain point, he would take his penis and tell me to let him put just the tip in my vagina. I was terrified as I had heard that sex hurt the first time. I kept asking if it was going to hurt and he kept assuring me that it would not. So he laid me on my side and he laid behind me and tried to put the tip of his penis in my vagina. I didn't know how to respond but I could feel him moving back and forth, behind me making these weird sounds. I could feel his penis between my thighs rubbing against them. But now in hindsight I think he thought he was penetrating me but he wasn't, so I just let him think he was until he finished and my thighs were all sticky. It grossed me out because I had no idea what that stick substance was. Of course, now that I am older, I know exactly what the sticky substance was.

Day in and day out while at school I would dread having to go home. I would get sick to my stomach, get a headache, or just didn't feel well. I would get this ire feeling all over. I didn't know if I was going to be molested that day or if I was going to be allowed to be free to be a child. I had begun distancing myself from people and keeping to myself, afraid that they would get to close and figure

46

out what's been going on at home. I was so tired and frustrated living this life but I was too scared to tell anyone. Nevertheless, the abuse remained, not daily but enough times whereas I was losing sleep because I didn't know the day, the time or the hour that I would be confronted and sexually abused. Not only was I sexually abused, mental abuse raised its ugly head as well. The mental abuse came into place when we would have to sleep in front of my family member house knowing we had a bed that we could sleep in, when we would have to sit in the car the whole entire day, doing nothing while my dad would be spending time with his buddies drinking and talking or when we couldn't get our hair done and we had to go to school the next day or even having to share the same clothes with your sibling because money was scarce. Then the name calling, anywhere from being called ugly, nappy headed, and dirty, it all played a toll on my mental state. Being physically and emotionally abused was a heavy burden to carry for anyone at any age.

I would excel in school with my grades as I was always exceeding and working above my grade level. I also played sports,

47

even the ones I did not like, as an outlet and to stay away from home as much as possible thinking this would stop the abuse. I tried to make my father proud hoping and wishing this would somehow convince him that he should stop doing what he has doing. Nevertheless, these tactics did not work at all. I only found myself tired and sleepy in the mornings because no matter what time I was done with sports and homework, if he wanted to molest me, he would do so no matter the time.

To make a long story short, eventually years later, I would get the help I needed to get out of this situation. Thanks to one of my siblings who was brave enough to let an adult person know what was going on at home right under their noses. Once the secret was out, things moved rather quickly. While at school, I was called out of class because a social worker wanted to speak with me. I didn't know what was going on as this was all a shock to me because at the time I did not know that my sibling had told anyone what was happening. Sitting there in front of this lady while she is explain why she was there talking with me, my heart was in my stomach. I was so scared and didn't know what to do or say. Should I deny everything? I had to muster up the courage to let my voice be heard. All I could do is cry. However, I took a deep breath, looked the social worker at her face with tears running down my face and told my truth. I felt like this was one of the hardest things I had to do, tell on my father! I was supposed to be able to go to him and tell on others, he was supposed to be my protector from the world. While telling my story I became overly nervous because it was close to the end of the day and I knew my father would be at the school to pick us up and take us home. Not knowing that the social worker was going to remove us from the home to keep me from harm. After about an hour or more of talking, we were told that we would be going to a foster home and were led to a waiting vehicle. While in the vehicle leaving the school, low and behold who did I see walking up to the school to pick us up. The molester! I ducked so that he would not see me as I was so terrified and thought to myself, "If he see us, these people have no idea, as they were going to have a fight on their hands because he was not going to allow

49

anyone to dare take his children from him." From that day forward, my life has never been the same.

Shantel Greer
Author/Jewelry Maker

"Deceitful Troy"

How did I miss so many signs? When God speaks, listen. Given the tools I was needed to see the light. Still I was blind, by L-O-V-E. For Shantise and Troy, life was good. After failing the Online Postal Exam, I secretly took the exam for him and passed. With my job at the hospital, and Troy's job at UPS we created a comfortable living together. We were a couple for 8 years, living together 7, and married 1-1/2. It wasn't until the I dos that things began to unravel. Or shall I say reveal.

I admit, yes, I had seen phone logs of unknown callers to me. Troy use to turn down rides to and from work claiming he did not want to bother me. He also would get up one hour earlier than needed to get to work. Who was I to question Troy for wanting to use public transportation, such as BART. Red flags were waving but the devil was invisibly busy. Keeping me blind to the fact.

Driving home from Hertz Rental Car agency, I noticed my husband left his backpack in my car. Normally no big deal. I looked at it and continued driving. Was the devil busy or was this God's plan? As I put my hand on top of the backpack, I felt a phone, now at this point I'm thinking how careless he was for leaving his phone. Not knowing how care, less he really was.

I got the phone out and to my surprise it was his old phone. "Now that's weird." I thought to myself. So, I plugged it in the charger port and turned it on. My heart was racing, breath got shorter, the lines on the road got blurry. I pulled over to collect myself. After pulling myself together, I proceeded to drive home. Those 20 minutes seemed like eternity.

The things I uncovered, the photos, emails and text!
I don't even remember parking. I walked in and saw my husband sitting upright watching television. Without thought, with rage I

jumped on the bed yelling, "WHAT DOES THIS MEAN?" I held the phone to his face demanding answers. Startled, he responded, "NOTHING." This means, "NOTHING."

Arguments flared for days as I continued to investigate. I started with checking emails. Nothing could prepare me for the truths that was about to unfold. The first thing I found was LGBT websites confirmations, Craigs list confirmations, that Troy had become a member of. Some of the websites were, Tinder, MocoSpace, and Tumblr, a few of many. Emails and photos from transgenders and Bitcoin accounts that were used to purchase sexual favors online. Hoping I would not be able to trace moneys spent. I combed over years of emails dating back to the year 2008. That was a whole year before we met.

Unfamiliar with The LGBT dialog, I struggled to know the meaning of some of the things I was reading. There were emails both to Troy and from Troy." DTF"!!! "I am hosting," But what does this mean? On the Tinder site his profile name was Trojanhorse227, Bisexual male "DTF" "Top" and "Bottom". All these emotions hit at once, I was frustrated, hurt, upset and furious. I questioned him again. This time presenting the evidence at hand. He had no choice but to confess. "I am intrigued with transgenders." I froze! I wanted to know the truth but at the same time, that's not what I wanted to hear. I sat on the side of the bed as I collected my thoughts. The room sat still for a moment. My mind ran crazily wild with visons and thoughts. I began to collect a mental list of questions to ask. Filled with disappointment I held the questions in. The next day, Troy came in from work. I was sitting on the side of the bed as if I had slept there last night. He dropped to his knees apologizing he said, "I am so sorry I hurt you. I AM intrigued with transgender and I enjoy sexual encounters with other men." I ask him, "Why didn't you tell me any of this before? Why did you even get married?" "I was selfish, and I did not want to let you go" he responded at this point, my mental note of questions began to flourish. My raging anger turned in to a full investigation. The first thing I did was to make an appointment and went to get checked out. Compulsively, I went to the doctors 3 times to check and

54

recheck. The Doctor assured me I was clear and advised me I did not need to recheck.

Too make light of this, I had to have a better understanding. The first question was what does all this mean? DTF, Hosting, Top, Bottom? Surprisingly I learned that DTF stood for, Down to Fuck. Hosting was the person whose house, hotel, or place one would meet up at. A Top is a male who prefers to be on top during sex and a bottom is a male who prefers to be on the bottom during sex. The next few days I plotted, planned, searched, researched and pondered. My feelings toggled between being angry and understanding. Troy had been this way many years and attempted to fight the feeling. He was dating women to cover up. He was a late bloomer as his family puts it. Now, I know why.

I remember this one time, when we fought in the bathroom. I had walked in on him while on the phone and he fought hard so I couldn't see his phone. I now realize he had been taking a picture of his private parts and probably sending it to one of his transgender hook ups. Yes! There were so many ignored signs! In another occasion, I dropped him off at work and an hour later, I got a call that he was in another city other than where he worked at. I called him and said, "I do not know who you are with or where you are but if I beat you home, all your stuff will be outside."

I remember asking him, "Are you with another woman?" He said NO and he put that on God. Well now I know the reason why he was able to say with a bold face that he was not with another woman. Because he was with other men. I made him stay on the phone as he left. He said, "alright you guys I am out!" I heard men voices.

There were times when our sex life was not so active. He would suffer from erectile dysfunction. When I confronted him, he assured it wasn't because he wasn't attracted to me. We even went to see a specialist who prescribed Viagra. The side effects were not good for Troy, so we had to discontinue them. Later finding that the Erectile Dysfunction syndrome he suffered from was common in gay males.

I continued my research. I even reached out to friends and

family members. (the telephone ringing) 'Hello?" "Omg auntie!! I cannot believe what you sent me!" I got a call from my nephew who is a transgender male. He is very prominent and reputable in the community. "Auntie I know all of these guys, Briar, Devonte, Christian and Delano. I will call them and call you back." "Thank you, nephew I will be waiting." I received that call, from my nephew. "Auntie, I am so sorry! He is out here. messing with all these men doing a lot. These guys know your business auntie. Dell says he knows Troy and they hang out. He said that Troy picks him up in the rental, even tells him that the rental is his." Now, for anybody that knew Shantise, they will tell you that I have a rental car fetish.

More and more started to come clear to me. I wanted to contact these guys. I begun with the two that my nephew was most familiar with.

Two of the guys he knew on a personal level. Christian. He knew Troy, very well. They met on Craigslist dating site for the LGBTQ community.

After my nephew reached out to, Christian. He voiced his concern. He worried about being exposed with Troy. He was the first one. I decided to contact him by email. In the email I included that I was aware he was sleeping with my husband; He was honest about the encounter with troy. He added that he did not know anything about me. That troy had been telling him that he was a single gay male. Christian apologized and begged me to not expose him. Then he gave detail.

Next on my List was Dell. I contacted him as he had admitted to my nephew that Troy use to pick him up in the rental cars and give him rides to and from Bart. Dell's story was different from Christians because he even knew where we lived and where troy worked. He admitted to sexual encounters, even in the cars. Plus, I had printed out photos from Troy's phone, email, and several off the gay website that Troy was a member of. Dell was in a few of them. His face, along with other body parts were in the photos. Both Troy and Dell were using emails to send photos between the two of them.

I continued to dig deeper. I copied everything. I copied photos, emails, and text. I even copied website chats. I kept the copies just in case I needed them for court. Who would have thought one electronic device could hold the answers to a person's whole life? Or should I say one's secret life? In Troy's phone I found emails dated back to 2008! There were Photos of so many men, that I could not count. These photos included ass shots, pictures of ass holes, photos of penises, and more pictures of men sucking on fake penises. There were Over 30 conversations with men on Craig's List over the years. Some were too graphic to describe. I also found numerous gay websites that Troy trolled on a regular. They included, the profiles he created using names like The Damager, Trojanhorse227 and savagelife9600.

Troy was at work when I texted him with, "Can I ask you a personal question?" He replied, "Yes, but not if you're going to expose me." Troy feared I would expose him not to the world but to his parents. I asked, "How did you get into sex with transgender?" He started out with a story that he met someone on mocospace, whom he thought at the time was a female. He continued to explain that he went on a one night-stand sex date. He claims it was dark and they had anal sex and he could not tell. Now I didn't believe a word out of his mouth. I did allow him to finish, as he said after they were done, they turned on the lights and it was then he found out that he was having sex with a man. He continues to state his shenanigans. And stated he was mad at first but admits he liked it from then on. I was in disbelief. Not to the fact that he was tricked but to the fact that he even came up with a lame story like that.

The More I knew the more I wanted to know. Briar! Now Briar when I contacted him through text wasn't so nice to me! I laughed. How can he be mad because I notified him that I was aware of him messing with my husband? I texted him and introduced myself. At first, he was cooperative admitting that he and Troy had sex before, ongoingly. But not lately. So, then I sent him some of our wedding photos. He quickly changed up, clearly to protect Troy. Saying that, "oh it's a different person where talking about." He even went through the efforts of trying to send me a fake photo of some other guy. Until I sent him a full photo of a copy of Troy's email. It was an email from Briar to Troy with a note and a full photo of Briar, and a photo of Briar's ass with him holding it open to expose how wide he was. Switching up again he texted, "we kicked it a few times, but we only had Oral." Another lie! I advised him that his lies would get him nothing, but a court ordered subpoena when I sue Troy for Pain suffering and mental anguish. He came clean. I did nothing wrong he stated I told him I was a gay male. He told me he was bi, and he was single. Now we are getting somewhere. Briar threatened to file a report on me. I laughed at him. Soooo you are reporting a curios wife? I encouraged him to do so, for expressing that will help publish what went on behind my back. "Please report me I can see it now" laughing as I texted back. "Gay man reports curios wife investigating husband's lover, because he slept with her husband behind her back." He replied, "well I would never have messed with him had I knew he had a partner."

Things happen for a reason. I never ask, God why? I only learn from my life lessons. I am grateful that God took that dark cloud out of my life. There is more than one lesson here. I lived with a man 6 whole years and never paid attention to the red flags. We had to get right by God and got married. It was not until than I saw the light of things. Wiser, Stronger and Unstoppable, I receive this lesson.

Special Presentation by Author Rachel E. Bills

"Terms of Endearment"

The story you are about to read is about a woman I know and love dearly. Her name is Angelina Denise Edwards, and she's my sister. I'm not sharing her story because she is my flesh and blood; I'm sharing it because her story is life-changing. Angie has lived a phenomenal life that most would consider a tragic death sentence. In fact, Angie has watched many of her own peers and a family member give up on life and choose death.

Born March 6, 1960, Angie grew up in Pittsburg, California; a small town in the East Bay Area. She is the third oldest of six children. Angie loved being active as a child. She was in girl scouts and the marching band in school. She has always been outgoing and the life of the party. She had plenty of friends who loved being around her because she made the atmosphere fun and funny. Angie was her daddy's little girl. Though she was the second daughter on her maternal side, she was the first daughter to her father. She enjoyed going to work with her dad; a privilege of the oldest to her dad. What more could a young child ask for? Friends, family to be daddy's little girl? Well, Angie's life would soon take a turn that would drastically change the course of her life forever.

On September 3, 1971, Angie lost the first man in her life who had ever loved her, her dad due to lung complications. Angie rarely spoke about how the grief of the loss made her feel. However, you can only imagine having someone so dear to you taken away. In fact, when Angie spoke of good times with her dad, her eyes would light up and the reflection of "Daddy's little girl" still sparkled.

Angie found herself demanding to know why God took her daddy? Sometimes, tears would creep up in her eyes, but she'd hurry and wipe them off before anyone could see. Angie refused to allow anyone to see that side of her. Instead, anyone who encountered her would get one of her two extremes: her joking around and making others laugh side, or her switchblade-carrying fighting-side. Angie lived in the ghetto, but she was not afraid to protect herself.

Sometimes, we just don't know what curveballs will be thrown into our lives. When we're young, we believe we have everything all figured out until reality proves us wrong. Lol. Then we reach our later-adult years and realize, "Oh crap! I'd better get things in order." Or, as in Angie's case, life happens and then our eyes are opened.

As I mentioned, Angie was one of those individuals who was carefree, outgoing and fun. She was the life of the party. As a teenager in the 70s, roller skating and music was the pastime. Among some of her favorites were Earth, Wind & Fire, The Brothers Johnson and of course the Isley Brothers. School was not something that was promoted in her household. In fact, Angie usually ditched school to hang out with her best friends. Like most of her friends at that time, house parties were Angie's main pastime. Her younger sister by three years would also sometimes come with her to hang out. Pittsburg was a small town where everyone who'd grown up knew each other from generation to generation. This is what made Pittsburg a love/hate place to live.

One day when she was 15, she met a 6 foot 2, tall, brown-skinned brother. He was just a couple of years older than Angie. They were familiar faces because they knew some of the same people; they'd just never really talked. But for some reason, this day would be the beginning of something FOREVER! So, this young man, checking out Angie's young but feisty curves, has one of his friends, who happens to know Angie, introduce him. Angie wasn't the least interested; after all, she had a few choices already. But her friend pressed her to at least talk to…Ricky. So, she did. He was nice and polite to her, although that's how it always starts off. But Angie could tell Ricky was different. He wasn't like all the other guys with fast talk and slick moves. He was also kind of cute with his tall, slim body and John Travolta butterfly shirt and bell bottoms.

Ricky and Angie hung out until it was time her to go home. Well, she really didn't have a curfew. But she wanted to make sure her younger siblings were okay. After her father had passed away, her mom got with this guy, James. James was nothing like Angie's dad. James was an alcoholic and abusive to Angie's mother. Angie often wondered who would her mom get with a guy like this after having a working man like her dad. After her mother had got with James, Angie found herself spending more time with friends and less at home. Of course, you couldn't blame a teenage girl for her actions when her home is dysfunctional. By this time, Angie and Ricky were inseparable. She'd become part of his family. Maybe the relationship started as a way of getting away from her family drama, but even when James was brutally killed, Angie and Ricky's relationship continued. Five years later, Angie gave birth to a baby girl, La'shona. La'shona is the apple of Angie's eye. Angie used to say that her baby sister (me) was the most beautiful baby she'd ever seen and that she'd never loved anyone more than her dad. But when La'shona was born, she didn't have to any anything. Her actions proved that La'shona was the most important thing in her life.

Ricky supported Angie no matter what she did. So, when her drug use increased more and more, he took care of La'shona, cooked, cleaned and did whatever he had to do to maintain the house. Angie fed her addiction mostly through boosting in stores and stealing. She often sold items out of own home and stole from family members. Most of her childhood friends were addicts as well, so her dysfunctional habits seemed normal.

THAT TURNING POINT

As time went on and coming around to the mid-80s, Angie's daughter was now in elementary school, and Angie's friends were starting to get sick from years of drug abuse. Angie began to realize the means to an end. She loved La'shona so much and didn't want to destroy her child's life, so she made sure La'shona was safe with Ricky's mother who also lived in Pittsburg and worked as a Teachers' Aide for many years. Angie knew that although she couldn't control her addiction, she could control her daughter's safety. La'shona's grandmother didn't change a word. She loved Angie like her own daughter. I believe that she understood and saw the love Angie had her La'shona she was a single mother, and Ricky was her only child,

Less than eight years later, Angie started experiencing pain in her abdomen. This went on for weeks. Angie even said later that she didn't realize that she wasn't urinating. She was with Ricky, and Angie began to have excruciating pain until she was doubled over and couldn't walk. Ricky quickly took her into emergency. Minutes later, the doctor

68

informed her that she was having kidney failure and that she was fortunate to have made it to the hospital when she did. Angie didn't like hospitals and rarely went for even regular checkups. So, her first reaction was, "No, I'm leaving." The doctors urged her to stay. They even asked for her next of kin (our mother) and informed her that if Angie left, she would die.

Angie had lost the function of one kidney and half of the other. She was hospitalized and given emergency dialysis treatment. Angie was only 29 years old.

THAT "BUT GOD" MOMENT

I remember going to sit with Angie at dialysis. I didn't have a car, so Ricky would pick me up. Angie went to dialysis in Concord (California) three days a week for three hours each time. I didn't have children at the time, so it was fun sitting with my sister and talking. Sometimes, she would fall asleep. So, I would sit and read her Enquire and Sun magazine. She sure did love those tabloids. Dialysis became her life.

It became Ricky's life too. I remember one day we were on our way to the hospital and an old song came on the radio. Though I didn't recognize the artist (or the song), I will never forget the words that Ricky song, "We've been together this love, we might as well stay together." Wow! You could feel that he was singing the song to Angie. I just sat listening to him sing more than the artist. The love he had for her was like no other I've ever seen. Though they weren't married, he exhibited a loving husband.

However, Angie still had urges for drugs, but she knew she had to change. Time had run out!

Angie had attended church, but it didn't hold her interest. But one day she was sitting in her living room, and she stumbled onto Robert Tilton. Back in the day, he was like TD Jakes and Joyce Meyers. It was a very popular Christian show. The show had praise and worship, outreach, preacher and powerful testimonies. Robert Tilton was known to really speak to his audience so that even the camera would zoom in closer to his face. Even as a young teenager, I would be moved by his words.

Well this day, Angie recalled him preaching really good, so she tuned in. What happened next was so awesome.

Robert Tilton preached in the prophetic, so he began to say, "There is someone out there with sick, kidney failure. If you want to be healed, come and touch the television." Angie immediately rose to her feet and laid both hands on the TV. She shared how tears began to flow down her cheeks.

Over the next years, Angie's life began to change drastically. She started going to church. She soon gave her life to Christ and became a faithful member of our family church. Soon, her family and friends began to see a difference in her. Angie watched many friends and even family members get sick from years of drug and alcohol abuse. Many of them died. She would talk to and encourage those who ended up on dialysis just like her. Through the years, she advised renal patients about self-care and the importance of following through doctor plans. I was so amazed and admired my sister because she'd turned her life around. She is so blessed to have lived these years on dialysis, raised her daughter, married the love of life and enjoyed life as a grandmother (a grandson). She didn't allow sickness to kill her spirit. She continued to be the life of the party, humorous as ever, but now, she was making the nurses, doctors and fellow patients laugh.

Now at 61 years, she and Ricky are still together. They finally married and made it official. Their daughter, La'shona, went on to graduate from Grambling University with a Bachelors in Criminal Justice. She also recently graduated with a Masters in Criminal Justice as well.

If asked, I'm sure Angie would agree that it was love for her daughter that sparked the change in her. But she gives all glory to God and boldly acknowledges how the chains of addiction were broken through Him. That it was Jesus Christ who sealed the deal.

I want to acknowledge to my sister Angelina Denise Edwards, who is one of the strongest, willful individuals I've never known. I love you sis!

About

the

Authors

La Wanda Marrero
(707) 646-1177
marrero.lawanda@gmail.com

La Wanda Marrero is a poet, Church Missionary and Leader of the Youth Ministry. She is an active community advocate and also works as an Associate Marriage & family Therapist.

La Wanda is the Founder of the nonprofit, Adnawal Inc. The organization promotes family physical, emotional, mental health and wellness through community collaborative partnerships, feeding programs, arts & crafts, and services for senior, adults and youth.

La Wanda published her first book, "Alice N Crackland" in 2008. After publishing, she realized writing was an essential tool in acknowledging, accepting and overcoming the challenges she faced as a child. She believed others could also benefit from learning to express themselves through the art of writing and pretense. This is when La Wanda's "Start Steppin" model was born. She now uses it to teach therapeutic writing groups through her book publishing company, "Unstoppable Book Publishing".

La Wanda explains, "In my addiction I affected many lives with a negative impact. My hope and desire are advocation to others through The Lord's grace. Having firsthand, knowledge of family dynamic and dysfunction motivates my passion to become a Licensed Marriage & Family Therapist and an advocate for writers. As I journey the road of redemption I desire to be a bridge to healing for those who want it."

Rachel E. Bills
(916) 399-3413
wovpublishingco@gmail.com

Rachel E. Bills is a native of the Bay Area, born and raised in Pittsburg, California. Rachel has worked in the administrative field for over 20 years and in the counseling field for about ten years. this includes mental health, addictive and Christian counseling.

Rachel holds a Bachelor of Science in Business Management and a Master's in Counseling/Marriage & Family Therapy. She is currently a registered Marriage and Family Therapist Intern in the state of California.

Rachel is also the Founder and Director of *Women of Virtue Org.;* an organization designed to improve the health and wellness of women, their families and community She believes the organization to be a divinely appointed assignment to serve the community by helping those in need to reach their full potential. She refers to the Power for 4-E's, Educate, Equip, Empower and Encourage as the key to help accomplish the mission of *Women of Virtue* and refers to herself as a "Transformational Specialist & Coach".

Rachel has experienced many trials and hardships. She is a toxic relationship survivor, has overcome depression, low self-esteem and anxiety. However, she explains with per personal and professional experience, she is determined to help women currently facing or recovering from similar circumstances live their best life. Rachel launched her own publishing company in 2017, Women of Virtue Publishing (WOV Publishing). Her desire is to provide coaching and tools to help women self-publish their own book, as well as, publish her own inspirational and self-help literatures. She is always looking for women who are ready to share their story.

Sharnice Perryman

ladysharnice@gmail.com

Pastor Sharnice is a Prophet to the Nations, Prayer Warrior, Exhorter, Author, Teacher and Preacher. Most importantly she loves God and His people. Her mission in life is to equip and empower the people of God to discover and walk in their purpose. She is a mother of four and a grandmother of two. The pain that she has endured and have had to overcome in life have birthed her out into true ministry. She has recently pastored alongside her husband (now ex-husband) in the city of Antioch for two years. While pastoring she had the opportunity to effect change in the lives of many people as well as a dying community. She is the founder of Ladies on Purpose, which is a Ministry that was birthed to assist men and women in discovering their purpose thru God's Word through the power of prayer and Deliverance. She is a survivor of domestic violence, abandonment, homelessness and divorce, and truly knows what it means to never give up. She has allowed life's challenges to make her and not break her. Pastor

Sharnice is passionate about helping people and she is a FireBrand she *incites change by taking radical actions to bring about that change in their lives*. Sharnice has her B.A Degree in Business Leadership, and is the creator of "Kingdom Dwellers" t-shirts Psalms 91. She is an author and the Pastor of Turn Around Ministries for Kingdom Living Church in Stockton, CA. God has ordained and purposed her to uniquely minister to the hearts of hurting men and women not only locally but internationally. She has been thru the war but is not wore torn, been through the fire but doesn't smell like smoke and she has allowed her pain to push her to her purpose. It is her humble desire to be used by God in total submission to His will.

Tene Kyles
ladytene11@gmail.com

Tene Kyles was born in Berkeley, CA via way of West Oakland however raised in Alameda, California, Tene Kyles is a mother, a grandmother and a published author. But most importantly she is a survivor of sexual assault and domestic abuse. Tene is currently focusing on her passion for violence against women and children, in particular the sexual victimization of children by family members. This will include the impact of incestual rape on women and the impact that it has on their mental and physical health. Tene is hoping by telling her story of strength and triumph that it will prevent sexual abuse and help survivors heal from the lasting effects of abuse. Knowing first -hand how traumatic rape and sexual assault is and the impact it has, Tene has become an advocate for survivors. Her purpose is to give a voice to those who are too afraid to speak.

Tene is currently living in Stockton Ca., where she is also

overcoming as a single mom by defying the stereotypes and stigma of being a divorcee. She is an asset to her family and her church where she serves faithfully. By writing her story she has FOUND HER STRENGTH AND HER VOICE.

Shantel Greer

Shantel Greer describes herself as "A happy soul", who enjoys life as it comes to her, "I live and I learn. I love laughter, family, cooking, and poetry writing."

Shantel was born in Berkeley, California. Her parents became home owners when she was very young and moved to Pittsburg, California.

Shantel grew up in church and a family-oriented home. She describes it as, "Well-rounded". She has 9 siblings; six men and four women.

Shantel also has a well-rounded education. She attended Los Medanos College in Pittsburg (California) where she studied General Education. She attended Chabot College in San Leandro (California) where she studied Activity Director Personnel and Martinez (California) Adult Education where she completed The Business Administrator program.

Shantel lost her mother at the age of 16 and found herself having to grew up real fast to help raise her younger siblings. She also became

83

a mother herself at a young age, raising two beautiful daughters as a single mom. She expresses, "I raised two of the most beautiful girls. And as I raised my own kids, I enjoyed helping my younger siblings navigate through grief, schooling, sports, and life's ups and downs."

Shantel is a loyal, dedicated and driven woman. She has spent the last 20 years working in the health care industry, where she enjoys caring for the elderly.

"I am a firm believer that we are here for a reason."

Book Excerpts

An original work written for "Unstoppable" (2020)

By La Wanda Marrero

Ephesians 6:12

For our struggle is not against flesh and blood, but against the rulers, against the authorities, against the powers of this dark world and against the spiritual forces of evil in the heavenly realms.

To make a difference one must be a difference by doing differently. I have grown diligent to present myself to the Lord in truth. My story is that I have been a part of the mess up and it is my vowel to the Lord to be a part of the cleanup. By the grace of God, I am who I became, and it is not in vain. Per God 's instruction my full armor is on, I am strong in the Lord and in the power of his might no matter what it appears like. I stand firm, grounded so when the day of evil and spiritual forces of unsurety comes against me I will not waiver but look to the heavens for my strength.

Sequel from Breaking Through Barriers

By Sharnice Perryman

"The Conclusion of the Matter"

Not the happy ending I was expecting, however I am accepting the will of God for my life concerning my life and marriage. Two and a half years ago when my husband abandoned the marriage and when I got the prophetic word that 'God was going to restore", I automatically assumed that He was referring to my marriage. Not so. He was referring to me. God was making me a promise that He would restore me back to where I was prior to the marriage. And He did just that.

To make it perfectly clear, I went to a church service the other night to support some friends of mine. At the end of the service the speaker was asking for a sacrificial offering. I did not have any cash on me so I borrowed a dollar from the person next to me. I was giving out of obedience totally not expecting anything. I put that dollar in the basket and the Woman of God took my hand to deliver a very harsh but necessary word. Her exact words were "Woman of God, you have been questioning God when is your husband coming back? He is NOT COMING BACK. God is saying that it is time for you to MOVE ON. You have prayed all you can pray and fought all you can fight. It is not your fault that he is choosing to walk in disobedience. You should have no regrets. Move on with your life and your ministry. You need to be pastoring again, God is gonna bless you and you will have love again. She spoke about my children and the pain they had to endure watching my heart being broken yet once again, and how God was going to heal even their hearts. Those words hit my spirit like a ton of bricks and they literally had to hold me up and then eventually lay me on the floor where all I could do was weep and sob. She pronounced healing and blessings over me and I got up off that floor with such a renewed since of freedom. I knew at that moment it was truly over and I was able to accept it and move on.

Prior to this happening I had given a three -day healing and prophetic revival. The last day of the revival the Prophet who was in charge of the service was just about to close out. He turned to me to give me the most powerful life changing word concerning my personal ministry and my personal life. As well as give me a great impartation form him and one other powerful woman of God who was there. Before he was done doing what God had instructed him to do and while I was laying on the floor a sobbing mess, under the Power of the Holy Ghost he spoke these words to me. He said "he is coming back". Immediately I knew he was referring to my husband. I began to weep even harder. As he continued to pray I heard a friend of mine say "he has already come back". I was thinking to myself, has this man entered into this church without me knowing? I was so confused and even more confused when I had gotten up and he was not there.

A few days had past and my friend who said that my husband was already back had asked to speak to meet with me. We met and she spilled all the tea concerning my now ex-husband. She said that her brother a very close friend of my husband had reached out to her concerning my ex-husband saying that he was homeless, sleeping in his car. He asked if she would help him by giving him a place to stay? Out of the kindness of her heart she had agreed. So that is what she meant the night of the revival when she had said he has already returned. He was their lurking around the church at the time of my revival. She said it was the worst mistake of her life and he was giving her pure hell, partially because he was unable to pay his rent and utilities along with undermining her authority with her church members. She said that apparently, he had a girlfriend as well and was bragging about how his divorce was final. I sat their listening in disbelief but at the same time thanking God that He would never leave me ignorant to the devil's devices. I was thanking God that His word is true, that he would prepare a table for you right in front of your enemy. I did not even ask for any of this, but He saw fit to give it to me.

I thought to myself, how much more God will I have to endure before you send him home and restore the marriage. I knew that based on the word that he was going to restore that I would still have to receive him back even on top of this added humiliation, and

I was still prepared to do so. That night I had a dream about my now ex-husband and the dark condition of his heart and his ill intentions when it came to my friend who was helping him. It just saddened me that he had become so low in his morals and sense of integrity. He had fallen so far from grace. Had she asked me I could have given her some insight on the person he had shown himself to be to me during the time of our split. Well their landlord tenant relationship did not work out and she had plans to evict him. Although God had used other means to remove him form her property. Here he was homeless, jobless, churchless, family-less, and just about friendless.

I could not believe that my now ex-husband would have rather be homeless than to just return back to his marriage. He was given a warning by a prophet to return home to the wife that God gave you or your life would come to ruin. I have seen it for my own eyes. That word has surly come to pass. After I had shared the word of release to my friend she felt free to share even more with me about my husband. I thought, my God there is more? She said that he was telling her and others vicious lies about me and our marriage trying to justify his heinous actions and discredit me as a person and woman of God. He didn't know how close me and this person had become over the past year. She had already gotten to know me as a friend and a confidant. I had never spoke badly about my husband to her. All she knew was that I was patiently and faithfully waiting for his return. But here he was bad mouthing me with hopes of making himself look credible. She said she told him she had not known me to be the person he was describing which I believe just infuriated him. I was thinking why he couldn't just depart in peace especially since it was his choice. Why try to come against me, what was the point. Then I thought he had to in order to justify his actions in the eyes of the people.

Pride has a way of taking people really low and will make them do demandable things. It will cause you to lose everything. My now ex-husband walked away from his wife, family and church unprovoked and unjustifiable. All because of pride and allowing his emotions to dictate how he would live. Instead of believing God and His word concerning his future. Him leaving the marriage only boils down to one thing. He was able to embrace the promise but not embrace the responsibilities that come with the promise. Marriage is an adjustment and adjustment require work. You must be willing to put the work in to reap the fruits of marriage. I am walking in the promises of God, not because I am better but because I am willing.

ISAIAH 40:31... But they that wait upon the Lord shall renew their strength; they shall mount up

with wings as eagles; they shall run, and not be weary; and they shall walk, and not faint.

Excerpt from. *"Restored: Healing from Brokenness"*

By Rachel E. Bills

(A 30-Day Devotional to be Releases in 2021)

"And the lord restored the fortunes of Job, when he had prayed for his friends. And the Lord gave Job twice as much as he had before. Job 42:10

"I looked toward the hills, which cometh my help."

As I sat in the small room, I was surrounded by others sharing the sorrows in their life that brought them there. One guy was there because he was diagnosed with an incurable disease that was slowly stealing his sight. One lady was there because as she mourned the loss of her beloved father, her family were more concerned with his estate. I anticipated what I was going to say, while thinking, "It's not that bad. All I have to say is what I'm feeling." As my turn approached, I closed my eyes and begin to open my mouth. Then I pushed out the words.."I'll pass."

...to be continued

"How to Know Love From Deceit"
Poem By Shantel Greer

Love to fault is always blind,

Always is to Joy inclined,

Lawless, winged and unconfined,

And breaks all chains from every mind.

Deceit from secrecy confined,

Lawful, caution and refined,

To everything but interest blind,

And Forge fetters for the mind.

I am not against the LGBTQ Community.

I am Only against the deceit.

Know the difference!!

About Women of Virtue Publishing

Women of Virtue Publishing was founded by Author Rachel E. Bills, which is a subsidiary of Women of Virtue Book Club. The book club was formed over 10 years ago and consisted of a small group of women reading inspirational books, meeting once a month for discussion and fellowship. The women were empowered and grow. Rachel, however, was not only empowered, but motivate to write and share her story.

In 2015, after moving to Sacramento, California, Rachel started a Women of Virtue Writing Group to support women who desired to write and share their story (just as she had done that same year). This time, the small group of women would meet up to support each other as fellow writers/Authors.

In 2017, Women of Virtue Publishing published its first book compilation, Stepping Out, Moving Forward. The compilation offered a platform for women to tell their story that would help others dealing with similar issues and traumas. To hopefully motivate them to share their story if they desired.

"Unstoppable" is the third compilation and its platform continues to inspire and encourage women that no matter what they go through, there is triumph at the end of the trial.

For more information about Women of Virtue Publishing
Contact them at:
(916) 399-3413
wovpublishingco@gmail.com

Made in the USA
Columbia, SC
13 February 2025

53769984R00071